The New User's Handbook To Android

The Essential Guide for New Smartphone Users and Beginners

The New User's Handbook To Android

Luis N. Murphy

TABLE OF CONTENT

The New User's Handbook To Android

Introduction to Android

What is Android?

Android is an open-source mobile operating system developed by Google. Launched in 2008, it was designed to power a wide variety of devices, particularly smartphones and tablets, but now extends to smart TVs, smartwatches, car infotainment systems, and even some home appliances. The key feature of Android is its adaptability and customization, allowing both manufacturers and users to modify aspects of the user interface and functionality.

Android's open-source nature means that device manufacturers—such as Samsung, Google, LG, and Sony—can create unique versions of Android (often called "skins" or "UI overlays") to differentiate their products while still running the core Android operating system.

Today, Android powers billions of devices worldwide, making it the most widely used mobile OS globally. Its vast ecosystem includes the Google Play Store, where users can download millions of apps to expand their device's functionality. Android's flexibility, user-friendliness, and extensive app ecosystem have made it a staple in mobile technology.

Key Features and Benefits

Android offers a robust suite of features that make it popular among users for both personal and professional use. Below are some of the key benefits and features that make Android stand out:

- **User-Friendly Interface**: Android's interface is intuitive, customizable, and designed to make navigation easy, even for beginners. Users can customize the layout, wallpaper, and themes and add widgets that display live information like weather, calendar events, and more directly on the home screen.

- **Customizability and Flexibility**: One of Android's greatest strengths is its level of customization. Users can change their launchers, icons, and layouts, allowing them to create a unique look and feel for their devices. There's also flexibility with app settings, display options, and other preferences.
- **Wide Range of Apps**: The Google Play Store offers millions of apps, ranging from productivity tools to games, media, and health apps. Android also supports third-party app stores, and users can sideload apps from other sources if they wish, giving them unparalleled access to diverse applications.
- **Google Integration**: As a Google product, Android seamlessly integrates

with Google services like Gmail, Google Drive, Google Photos, and Google Maps. This integration ensures that users can sync their data across devices and access it anytime, making productivity and data management more efficient.

- **Multitasking Capabilities**: Android allows users to switch between apps easily and even use split-screen mode for multitasking. Picture-in-Picture mode lets users continue watching a video while browsing or performing other tasks.

- **Regular Updates and Security**: Google releases regular updates to improve Android's performance, introduce new features, and enhance security. The Google Play Protect service, integrated within Android, scans apps for malware to keep devices safe from malicious content.

- **Voice Assistant and AI Integration**: Google Assistant, integrated into Android, uses AI to perform tasks, set reminders, answer questions, and even control smart home devices. This makes it easy for users to use their device hands-free or find answers to questions quickly.

- **Compatibility with a Wide Range of Devices**: Android runs on devices at various price points, offering options for every budget. Users can choose from a variety of models, from budget-friendly options to high-end flagship devices with cutting-edge technology.

Android Versions Overview

Android has evolved significantly over the years, with each new version bringing improved features, security updates, and interface changes. Google used dessert names for versions until Android 10, after which it switched to a numerical naming convention. Here's an overview of some notable Android versions:

- **Android 1.0 – 2.3**: These early versions focused on establishing the basic features of Android, such as support for Google services, a simple interface, and basic smartphone functionalities.

- **Android 4.0 Ice Cream Sandwich**: Introduced a unified UI for both phones and tablets, improving the visual appeal of Android and adding features like facial recognition for unlocking the device.
- **Android 5.0 Lollipop**: This update introduced the "Material Design" language, which changed the interface with colorful visuals, shadows, and responsive animations.
- **Android 6.0 Marshmallow**: Focused on app permissions, improved battery life with Doze mode, and introduced the Google Now on Tap feature.
- **Android 7.0 Nougat**: Introduced split-screen mode, improved notifications, and new emoji.
- **Android 8.0 Oreo**: Added Picture-in-Picture mode, auto-fill for passwords, notification channels, and improved speed and security.

- **Android 9 Pie**: Focused on digital wellbeing, with tools to help users manage screen time, along with new gesture-based navigation.
- **Android 10**: The first version to drop the dessert name, Android 10 introduced dark mode, enhanced privacy controls, and Focus Mode for better concentration.
- **Android 11**: Improved media controls, a conversation section in notifications, and better support for smart home devices.
- **Android 12**: Brought the "Material You" design language, allowing users to customize colors, shapes, and styles across the OS based on their wallpaper colors.
- **Android 13 and Beyond**: Continued to improve on customization, privacy, and seamless device integration.

Each Android update is designed to keep the OS secure, feature-rich, and compatible with evolving user needs. Android's commitment to regular updates and improvements keeps it relevant in a fast-paced tech world.

Getting Started: Setting Up Your Device

Setting up an Android device for the first time is straightforward, with prompts to guide users through each step. Here's a basic guide to getting started:

- **1. Power On and Select Language**: Turn on your device and select your preferred language from the options provided.
- **2. Connect to Wi-Fi**: Connect to a Wi-Fi network to ensure your device can download any necessary updates and sync with your Google account.
- **3. Sign in or Create a Google Account**: You'll need a Google account to access most Android features, including the Google Play Store. You can either sign in

with an existing account or create a new one.

- **4. Restore or Set Up as New**: If you're coming from another Android device, you can restore your apps and settings from a previous backup. If this is your first device, you can choose to set it up as new.
- **5. Security Settings**: Set up a screen lock with a PIN, pattern, or password, and configure fingerprint or face recognition if your device supports it.
- **6. Customize Device Settings**: You'll be prompted to customize settings for app permissions, notifications, and privacy. This is a good time to review and adjust these settings to fit your preferences.
- **7. Install Essential Apps**: Once set up, you can start downloading apps from the Google Play Store. Popular apps for messaging, social media, and productivity are often recommended on the home screen.
- **8. Explore and Personalize**: After initial setup, explore your device to customize it.

Adjust the wallpaper, organize apps, and explore Google Assistant to make the device feel like yours.

Starting with these steps will ensure that your Android device is set up properly and personalized to your preferences. Each Android device may have some unique steps due to differences in manufacturer interfaces, but these general guidelines apply to all Android setups.

Basic Navigation and Interface

Understanding the Home Screen, Apps, and Widgets

The home screen is the central hub of an Android device, acting as both a navigation tool and a customizable workspace. Let's break down its key elements:

- **Home Screen Layout**: Android's home screen typically consists of multiple "pages" that can be swiped through horizontally. Each page can house app icons, widgets, and folders, which users can organize to their liking.

- **App Icons**: The app icons on the home screen act as shortcuts to open specific apps. You can add or remove these icons to create a personalized layout. Access all apps by swiping up from the bottom (on most devices) to reveal the app drawer, where every installed app is located.
- **Widgets**: Widgets are mini-applications that display live information directly on the home screen. Popular widgets include weather, calendar events, news updates, and music controls. To add a widget, press and hold on an empty area of the home screen, select "Widgets," and choose from the available options. Widgets can also be resized or moved around to fit your layout.
- **Folders**: To create folders and keep your home screen organized, drag one app icon onto another. This will create a new folder that can hold multiple apps. Folders can be renamed to make it easy to categorize apps, such as "Social Media," "Productivity," or "Games."

- **Dock and App Drawer**: Most Android devices have a "dock" at the bottom of the home screen. This dock remains static as you swipe between home screen pages, allowing quick access to essential apps like Phone, Messages, and Browser. The app drawer can be accessed by swiping up from the bottom or tapping a dedicated button, depending on the device.

With these customizable elements, users can set up their home screens to maximize ease of access, functionality, and personal style.

Notification Panel and Quick Settings

The notification panel and quick settings are essential tools for managing alerts, settings, and other actions without opening individual apps.

- **Accessing the Notification Panel**: To access the notification panel, swipe down

from the top of the screen. Here, you'll
see recent notifications from apps like
Messages, Email, and social media.
Notifications can be interacted with
directly from the panel, such as replying
to messages, dismissing reminders, or
controlling media playback.

- **Interacting with Notifications**:
Notifications can be expanded by swiping
down on each one, revealing additional
options (like a "Reply" button for
messages). Swiping a notification to the
left or right will clear it from the panel.
Long-pressing on a notification offers
options to adjust its settings, such as
turning off notifications from that specific
app.
- **Quick Settings**: Below or within the
notification panel is the quick settings
menu, where users can toggle settings like
Wi-Fi, Bluetooth, Do Not Disturb,
Airplane Mode, and Mobile Data. Quick
settings often include a brightness slider

and shortcuts for battery saver, flashlight, and screen rotation.

- **Editing Quick Settings**: Most Android devices allow you to customize quick settings by dragging down the panel completely and tapping the "Edit" or "Pencil" icon. This lets you add or remove shortcuts based on your preferences.

The notification panel and quick settings simplify multitasking by making common actions accessible from anywhere, saving time and reducing the need to open the settings app.

Using Gesture and Button Navigation

Android offers two main navigation styles: **gesture navigation** and **button navigation**. Each option has its own learning curve, but they're both intuitive once you get familiar with them.

- **Gesture Navigation**:
  - Gesture navigation removes physical or on-screen buttons and relies on swiping gestures for navigating the device. This option is common on newer devices and helps maximize screen space.
  - **Going Home**: Swipe up from the bottom of the screen.
  - **Opening Recent Apps**: Swipe up from the bottom and pause in the middle of the screen to view recently used apps.
  - **Going Back**: Swipe from the left or right edge of the screen to go back to the previous screen.
  - **Switching Apps Quickly**: Swipe left or right on the bottom edge of the screen to switch between recently used apps.
  - **Accessing Google Assistant**: Swipe up diagonally from the bottom corners to launch Google Assistant.

- **Button Navigation**:
  - Button navigation uses three main buttons at the bottom of the screen, which is still common on many Android devices.
  - **Home Button**: The central button takes you back to the home screen from any app.
  - **Back Button**: The back button (usually on the left) allows you to go back one step in any app or exit the app.
  - **Recent Apps Button**: The right button (or a long-press on the home button in some devices) brings up the recent apps view, where you can switch between open applications or swipe them away to close.
- **Choosing Navigation Style**: To choose between gesture and button navigation, go to **Settings** > **System** > **Gestures** > **System Navigation** (on most devices). This allows users to toggle between

gestures and buttons based on their preference.

Learning to navigate using gestures can take some practice, but it's designed to create a more fluid experience on the device, especially for those with larger screens.

Lock Screen and Security Options

Android offers various security features to help protect your data, starting with the lock screen. Here's an overview of key security options:

- **Lock Screen Basics**: The lock screen is the first screen displayed when waking up the device. It usually displays essential information like the date, time, and notification previews. From the lock screen, users can access the camera by swiping or long-pressing, depending on the device.

- **Lock Screen Methods**: Android devices offer several options to secure the lock screen, including:
  - **Swipe**: This is the most basic option, requiring no security. Swiping unlocks the device immediately.
  - **Pattern**: A pattern lock lets you draw a specific pattern on a grid. It's a good balance between ease and security.
  - **PIN**: A numerical passcode, similar to an ATM PIN, provides a higher level of security than a pattern.
  - **Password**: The most secure option, a password, requires alphanumeric input and is typically harder to guess.
  - **Biometric Options**: Many devices now support **fingerprint scanning** and **facial recognition**, allowing users to unlock their device quickly without entering a pattern, PIN, or

password. Biometric options are secure and convenient for daily use.

- **Advanced Lock Screen Security**:
  - ○ **Smart Lock**: Android's **Smart Lock** feature allows the device to stay unlocked in trusted situations, such as when it's in a trusted location (like home), connected to a trusted Bluetooth device, or when it detects that it's being carried. This feature is found under **Settings > Security > Smart Lock**.
  - ○ **Lock Screen Notifications**: By default, notifications can appear on the lock screen. You can customize whether these are fully visible, partially hidden, or entirely turned off by going to **Settings > Notifications > Lock screen**. This option can help protect sensitive information from being visible to others.
- **Additional Security Features**:

- ○ **Find My Device**: Android has a built-in **Find My Device** feature that allows you to locate, lock, or erase your device remotely if it's lost or stolen. This can be accessed via **Settings** > **Security** > **Find My Device**. You can also use the "Find My Device" app or website to perform these actions.
- ○ **App Lock**: Some devices support app locks that protect specific apps with a password or biometric security, adding an extra layer of privacy.
- ○ **Google Play Protect**: This feature continuously scans apps on your device and apps you download from the Play Store for potential security threats. It ensures that malware or suspicious activities are flagged before they can harm the device.
- **Setting Up a Secure Device**:
  - ○ A secure Android device should at least have a lock screen PIN or

    pattern, with biometric security enabled for quick access.

- Regularly review app permissions and privacy settings to make sure that each app has access only to necessary information.
- Enable automatic updates to ensure your device has the latest security patches and features.

Lock screen security not only protects your device from unauthorized access but also helps safeguard personal data, making it essential for every Android user to implement a security option that fits their comfort level.

Customizing Your Device

Customizing your Android device is a fun and practical way to make it feel uniquely yours. From wallpapers and themes to organizing apps and adjusting display settings, Android offers numerous ways to tailor your device to your preferences and needs. Let's explore how to make the most of these customization options.

Changing Wallpaper and Themes

One of the simplest ways to make your device feel personal is by changing the wallpaper or theme. This not only freshens up your screen but also allows you to express your style.

- **Changing Wallpaper**:
  - ○ **Accessing Wallpaper Options**: Press and hold an empty space on your home screen, then tap "Wallpapers" or "Wallpaper & Style." You'll see options for pre-installed wallpapers, live wallpapers, or the ability to choose an image from your gallery.
  - ○ **Selecting a Wallpaper**: Browse through the available categories like "Nature," "Cityscapes," or "Abstract" to find one you like. Select the image, then choose to set it as the wallpaper for either the home screen, the lock screen, or both.
  - ○ **Using Your Photos**: You can set personal photos or images as wallpapers. Tap on "My photos" to choose from images in your gallery,

then adjust the positioning to make
sure the focus is where you want it.
- ○ **Live Wallpapers**: Android supports
  live wallpapers—animated
  backgrounds that add a dynamic
  touch. They may use more battery,
  but they can bring a unique look to
  your device.
- **Changing Themes**:
  - ○ **Device Themes**: Some Android
    versions come with built-in themes
    that allow you to change the entire
    look of the system UI, including
    colors, icons, and text styles. To
    find these options, go to **Settings** >
    Display > **Theme** (or **Wallpaper &
    Style**).
  - ○ **Third-Party Themes**: If your
    device supports it, you may also
    find themes in the Play Store. These
    can apply new icons, wallpapers,
    fonts, and even animations to create
    a unified look. Popular launchers
    like Nova Launcher and Microsoft

Launcher allow extensive theme customization.

- ○ **Material You**: Starting with Android 12, Google introduced "Material You," a dynamic color theme that changes based on your wallpaper. This feature allows you to match system colors with your wallpaper, giving the interface a cohesive look. You can adjust these colors in **Settings** > **Wallpaper & Style**.

Customizing wallpapers and themes is a quick and easy way to bring personality to your device, making it more visually appealing and tailored to your taste.

Organizing Apps and Folders

A well-organized home screen improves efficiency and allows you to find apps faster. Organizing apps into folders and placing commonly used apps where they're easy to access can help you navigate the device more effectively.

- **Adding Apps to the Home Screen**:
  - ○ **Accessing the App Drawer**: Swipe up from the bottom of the screen to access the app drawer, which contains all installed apps. You can move any app icon to the home screen by pressing and holding the icon, then dragging it to the desired position.
  - ○ **Dock Placement**: Place frequently used apps, like Phone, Messages, or Browser, in the dock at the bottom of the home screen for easy access. The dock remains visible across all home screen pages, making it ideal for essential apps.
- **Creating Folders**:
  - ○ **Grouping Apps Together**: To create a folder, drag one app icon on top of another. This will

automatically create a folder
containing both apps.

- o **Renaming Folders**: Tap the folder
  to open it, then tap "Unnamed
  Folder" (or the default name) to
  rename it. You could categorize
  apps by function, such as "Social
  Media," "Work," "Games," or
  "Entertainment."

- o **Rearranging Folder Contents**:
  Within a folder, apps can be
  rearranged by pressing and
  dragging them to the desired
  position. This is useful if you want
  certain apps within a folder to
  appear at the top.

- **Organizing Multiple Home Screens**:
  - o **Adding and Removing Pages**:
    Most Android devices allow you to
    add multiple home screen pages. To
    add a page, drag an app to the edge
    of the screen, and a new page will
    be created. To remove a page,
    delete or drag all apps off of it.

○ **Arranging Pages**: Rearrange the order of your home screen pages by pressing and holding an empty area, then dragging the pages to reorder them.

A well-organized home screen setup can save time and reduce frustration when looking for apps, particularly if you're someone who keeps many apps installed.

Adjusting Sound, Display, and Accessibility Settings

Android's settings allow you to adjust sound and display options for a personalized experience and make the device more accessible. Let's go over some of the most useful settings.

- **Sound Settings**:
  - ○ **Accessing Sound Settings**: Go to **Settings > Sound & Vibration** to access various sound settings.

- ○ **Ringtones and Notification Sounds**: Customize the ringtone and notification sounds by selecting **Ringtone** and **Notification sound** options. You can choose from default sounds or add your own.
- ○ **Volume Controls**: Adjust media, call, and notification volumes independently. This allows you to lower ringtone volume while keeping media loud, for example.
- ○ **Do Not Disturb**: Enable Do Not Disturb mode to silence calls, messages, and notifications during specific times or events. You can customize it to allow calls from certain contacts or enable alarms while blocking other sounds.
- **Display Settings**:
  - ○ **Brightness**: Adjust screen brightness manually or enable **Adaptive Brightness**, which automatically adjusts based on ambient light conditions.

- ○ **Screen Timeout**: Change the screen timeout setting to determine how long the device stays on before locking. Longer timeouts can be convenient, but shorter ones save battery life.
- ○ **Font and Display Size**: Go to **Settings** > **Display** > **Font size** or **Display size** to make text and icons larger or smaller. This can improve readability and usability for those with vision difficulties.
- **Accessibility Settings**:
  - ○ **Magnification**: Android includes a magnification feature that allows users to zoom in on parts of the screen. Enable this in **Settings** > **Accessibility** > **Magnification**.
  - ○ **Color Correction and Inversion**: For those with color blindness, Android offers color correction and color inversion options in **Settings** > **Accessibility** > **Color correction**.

○ **TalkBack**: Android's screen reader, TalkBack, provides spoken feedback for users with visual impairments. It can be enabled under **Settings > Accessibility > TalkBack**.

○ **Accessibility Shortcuts**: Customize shortcuts for accessibility tools, like holding down both volume buttons to launch TalkBack or magnification.

These sound, display, and accessibility settings can make your Android device more comfortable to use, improving your experience based on your individual needs.

Using Dark Mode and Night Light

Dark Mode and Night Light are display options designed to reduce eye strain, improve readability, and conserve battery life. Both modes can be enabled manually or set to activate automatically based on a schedule.

- **Dark Mode**:
  - **Benefits of Dark Mode**: Dark Mode is popular for its eye strain reduction, especially in low-light environments, and for saving battery on devices with OLED screens. It changes the interface from light to dark colors, affecting system apps and compatible third-party apps.
  - **Activating Dark Mode**: You can enable Dark Mode from **Settings** > **Display** > **Dark theme**. You can choose to activate it immediately or schedule it to turn on automatically at night.
  - **App-Specific Dark Mode**: Many apps offer independent dark mode settings. For example, in apps like YouTube, Gmail, and Chrome, you can go into each app's settings to

enable Dark Mode regardless of
your system settings.

- **Night Light**:
    - ○ **What is Night Light?** Night Light,
      also known as "Blue Light Filter"
      on some devices, reduces the
      amount of blue light emitted by the
      screen. Studies suggest that blue
      light can disrupt sleep, so this
      feature adds a warm tint to the
      display, making it easier on the
      eyes, especially before bedtime.
    - ○ **Turning on Night Light**: Go to
      Settings > **Display** > **Night Light**
      to enable it. You can adjust the
      intensity of the filter and set a
      schedule for it to activate
      automatically, either from sunset to
      sunrise or during custom hours.
    - ○ **Using Night Light with Dark
      Mode**: You can use Night Light and
      Dark Mode together for maximum
      eye comfort, especially in dim
      lighting. While Dark Mode reduces

glare and brightness, Night Light reduces blue light, creating a softer viewing experience.

Both Dark Mode and Night Light contribute to a more comfortable, customizable viewing experience, particularly beneficial for users who spend extended time on their devices.

Essential Android Apps

Android devices come equipped with an array of apps that are essential for daily use and productivity. These apps, especially Google's core services, form the backbone of the Android experience, providing tools for communication, navigation, organization, and more. Additionally, exploring alternative apps allows you to further personalize your experience. This section will guide you through these essential apps and help you make the most of their features.

Introduction to Google Apps

Google apps are pre-installed on most Android devices and offer a suite of essential services that are highly integrated with the Android operating system. Let's take a closer look at some of the most commonly used Google apps and their functionality.

- **Play Store**:
  - ○ **What is the Play Store?** The Google Play Store is the primary marketplace for downloading apps, games, movies, books, and more on Android devices. It's essential for discovering new apps, updating existing ones, and managing subscriptions.
  - ○ **Navigating the Play Store**: The Play Store home page features recommendations and popular apps in various categories, such as "Top Free," "Top Grossing," and "Editor's Choice." You can search for specific apps using the search bar or explore by category.

- ○ **Managing Downloads and Updates**: To view or manage your apps, tap on your profile icon in the top-right corner, select "Manage apps & device," and navigate to "Updates" or "Installed." Here, you can update apps, view permissions, and remove any apps you no longer use.
- **Gmail**:
  - ○ **Features of Gmail**: Gmail is Google's email service, known for its user-friendly interface, spam filtering, and seamless integration with other Google services. You can manage multiple email accounts within Gmail, including accounts from other providers like Yahoo or Outlook.
  - ○ **Managing Inbox and Labels**: Gmail organizes emails by labels (e.g., Primary, Social, Promotions). You can customize labels to organize emails according to your

preferences. Additionally, features like snoozing, starring, and archiving help you manage and prioritize your inbox.

- ○ **Customizing Notifications**: You can configure Gmail notifications based on importance, so you only receive alerts for priority messages, reducing notification overload.
- **Google Maps**:
  - ○ **Navigation and Real-Time Traffic**: Google Maps offers turn-by-turn navigation for driving, walking, biking, and public transport. It provides real-time traffic data, road closures, and alternative route options to get you to your destination quickly.
  - ○ **Nearby Locations and Reviews**: Use Google Maps to explore nearby restaurants, hotels, and attractions. User reviews, photos, and ratings can help you decide where to go,

and you can save favorite spots for
easy access later.

○ **Offline Maps**: Download maps for
offline use, which is ideal for travel
or areas with limited internet.
Simply search for an area, select
"Download," and save it for future
use.

- **Google Photos**:
  ○ **Photo Storage and Organization**:
  Google Photos provides unlimited
  storage (with some restrictions) for
  photos and videos. It organizes
  media by people, places, and things,
  making it easy to locate images.

  ○ **Editing and Sharing**: Google
  Photos includes basic editing tools,
  filters, and collage options. It also
  simplifies sharing images with
  others, allowing you to create
  shared albums and send links for
  easy viewing.

  ○ **Backup and Sync**: Enable backup
  to automatically sync photos from

your device to Google Photos, ensuring they're safe and accessible from any device.

- **Google Drive**:
  - **Cloud Storage and Collaboration**: Google Drive offers cloud storage for files, making it easy to save, share, and collaborate on documents. It integrates with Google Docs, Sheets, and Slides, which can be accessed and edited directly within Drive.
  - **Organizing Files**: Drive allows you to organize files into folders, set permissions for shared files, and sync content across devices. It's particularly useful for accessing important files from anywhere.
- **YouTube**:
  - **Streaming Video Content**: YouTube is a major video platform for streaming content, from music videos and educational channels to vlogs and tutorials. Users can

subscribe to channels, create
playlists, and explore a wide variety
of content based on personal
interests.

- **YouTube Premium**: For an ad-free
experience, YouTube offers a paid
subscription that includes offline
downloads, background play, and
access to YouTube Music, Google's
dedicated music streaming service.

Together, these Google apps form a
comprehensive toolkit for communication,
media, and productivity. With the power of
Google's cloud services, they ensure seamless
access to your data and content across devices.

Messaging and Calling

Communication apps are central to any
smartphone experience. Android comes with
Google's messaging and calling apps by default,

which offer rich features and high compatibility across devices.

- **Google Messages**:
  - ○ **SMS and RCS Support**: Google Messages supports both SMS and RCS (Rich Communication Services) messaging, providing a more feature-rich experience similar to iMessage. With RCS, users can send high-resolution photos, see read receipts, and view typing indicators.
  - ○ **Group Messaging**: Group messaging allows users to send messages to multiple people simultaneously. Each participant can see responses from others, making it ideal for planning events or staying connected with friends.
  - ○ **Smart Reply and Chat Features**: Messages offers "Smart Reply" suggestions based on the context of your conversation, helping you

respond quickly. Additionally, you can use stickers, GIFs, and emojis to add more personality to chats.

- **Phone App**:
  - **Making Calls and Managing Voicemail**: The Google Phone app offers standard calling features, along with visual voicemail and call history. It's designed to be simple and intuitive, providing users with clear options for managing missed calls and voicemails.
  - **Caller ID and Spam Protection**: The Phone app includes built-in caller ID and spam protection, warning you of suspected spam calls before answering. This feature helps users avoid scams and unwanted interruptions.
  - **Favorites and Call Blocking**: Add frequently called contacts to your "Favorites" for easy access. The app also supports call blocking, so

you can avoid persistent spam numbers or unwanted calls.

These default apps provide a smooth and secure communication experience on Android devices. However, third-party messaging and calling apps like WhatsApp, Signal, and Skype are also popular and widely available on the Play Store.

Managing Contacts and Calendar

Keeping track of contacts and staying organized with a calendar are key components of productivity on Android. Google's Contacts and Calendar apps provide these functions with useful features and easy integration.

- **Google Contacts**:
  - **Adding and Organizing Contacts**: The Contacts app allows you to store and organize all your contacts. You can add email addresses, phone numbers, birthdays, and notes,

helping you keep detailed
information for each person.
- ○ **Syncing Contacts**: Contacts are
  synced across devices when linked
  to your Google account, making it
  easy to access contact information
  from any device logged into the
  same account.
- ○ **Merging Duplicates and Backup**:
  If you have duplicate contacts, the
  Contacts app can automatically
  detect and merge them. It also
  offers an option to backup contacts
  to Google's cloud, ensuring they're
  safe in case of device loss.
- • **Google Calendar**:
  - ○ **Event Creation and Reminders**:
    Calendar allows you to create
    events, set reminders, and schedule
    tasks. You can set up recurring
    events, such as weekly meetings,
    and add detailed notes to each
    event.

- ○ **Shared Calendars and Collaboration**: Google Calendar lets you create and share calendars with others, making it easier to coordinate schedules. For example, you can have a shared calendar with family or colleagues for group events.
- ○ **Calendar Widgets and Syncing**: Calendar widgets allow you to view upcoming events directly on your home screen. Additionally, all events are synced across devices, so you can access your schedule from any device with your Google account.

Managing contacts and keeping an organized calendar help streamline daily life, ensuring you never miss important events or lose touch with contacts.

Exploring Alternative App Options

Android's open platform allows you to explore countless third-party apps, offering flexibility and personalization beyond the default apps. Here are some popular alternative options for key functions:

- **Messaging**:
    - **WhatsApp**: A globally popular messaging app with end-to-end encryption, supporting text, voice, video calls, and group chats.
    - **Signal**: A secure messaging app focused on privacy, offering encrypted messaging and calling with robust data protection.
    - **Telegram**: Known for its high-speed messaging and group support, Telegram also offers public channels, file sharing, and customizable themes.
- **Calling**:
    - **Skype**: A versatile app for making video and voice calls over the

internet, commonly used for business and international communication.

- **Viber**: Another popular calling app with international call options, supporting encrypted chats and video calls.

- **Email**:
  - **Microsoft Outlook**: Combines email, calendar, and contacts in one app, with integration for both personal and work accounts.
  - **ProtonMail**: A secure email provider with a focus on privacy, offering end-to-end encryption and a strong privacy policy.

- **Navigation**:
  - **Waze**: An alternative to Google Maps, Waze provides community-sourced traffic information, making it ideal for real-time traffic alerts and navigation.

○ **HERE WeGo**: A navigation app with offline maps and local transit information, useful for travelers and offline use.

Exploring alternative apps allows you to find ones that fit your specific needs, preferences, and values, from privacy to usability.

Connecting and Syncing Devices

Modern Android devices are designed to seamlessly connect and synchronize with a variety of other devices and services, enhancing productivity, entertainment, and convenience. Whether you're using Bluetooth for wireless audio, syncing data with cloud storage, pairing with wearables, or integrating your device with your car, Android offers versatile options to keep you connected.

Bluetooth, Wi-Fi, and NFC Basics

Android's connectivity features, like Bluetooth, Wi-Fi, and NFC (Near Field Communication), allow you to transfer data, pair with devices, and access the internet.

- **Bluetooth**:
  - **What is Bluetooth?** Bluetooth is a wireless technology used for short-range communication between devices. You can use Bluetooth to connect with headphones, speakers, fitness trackers, or even share files with nearby devices.
  - **How to Pair Devices**: To enable Bluetooth, go to **Settings** > **Connected devices** > **Connection preferences** > **Bluetooth**, and turn it on. Once enabled, your device will start searching for nearby devices. Select the device you want to connect with, confirm any

pairing prompts, and your devices will be linked.

- **Bluetooth Profiles and Features**: Android supports various Bluetooth profiles for different functionalities, including A2DP for high-quality audio streaming, HID for wireless keyboards, and AVRCP for remote control of audio playback. Ensure your Bluetooth device supports the necessary profile for the best experience.

- **Wi-Fi**:
  - **Connecting to Wi-Fi Networks**: Wi-Fi provides a high-speed connection to the internet and allows data transfer without using mobile data. To connect, go to **Settings** > **Network & internet** > **Wi-Fi**, then select a network. Enter the password if required.
  - **Wi-Fi Direct**: Wi-Fi Direct is a feature that enables device-to-device connections

without an access point. It can be used to transfer files or play media on other devices, like smart TVs. Access it under **Wi-Fi settings** if your device supports it.

- ○ **Wi-Fi Hotspot**: Android devices can act as a Wi-Fi hotspot, allowing other devices to connect and use the mobile data connection. Set this up under **Settings** > **Network & internet** > **Hotspot & tethering**.
- **NFC (Near Field Communication)**:
  - ○ **How NFC Works**: NFC allows for short-range communication between compatible devices (up to a few centimeters). It's commonly used for contactless payments and quick data transfers.
  - ○ **Setting Up NFC**: Go to **Settings** > **Connected devices** > **Connection preferences** > **NFC** to enable it. Place your Android device near another NFC-enabled device or terminal to initiate a connection.

○ **Uses of NFC**: NFC is primarily used for payments through services like Google Pay, as well as for sharing files, connecting with compatible accessories, and scanning NFC tags.

These wireless technologies enhance your device's connectivity and make it possible to link with a variety of devices and services for a more integrated experience.

Setting Up Cloud Storage and Backup

Cloud storage and backup are essential for safeguarding your data and ensuring you can access your information from multiple devices. Google offers built-in cloud storage and backup solutions for Android, simplifying the process.

- **Google Drive**:

- o **Storage and File Management**: Google Drive provides 15GB of free cloud storage, shared across Google services. To access it, open the Drive app, where you can upload files, organize folders, and manage your storage.
- o **Sharing and Collaboration**: Google Drive allows you to share files or folders with others, making it ideal for collaboration. You can set sharing permissions to control who can view, comment, or edit files.
- o **Automatic Syncing**: Drive syncs automatically across devices with your Google account. Any changes you make on one device appear on others signed into the same account.
- **Google Photos Backup**:
  - o **Automatic Photo Backup**: Google Photos allows you to back up images and videos automatically. Go to **Google Photos** > **Settings** >

Back up & sync to enable this feature, ensuring your media is safely stored in the cloud.

○ **Storage Options**: Google Photos offers high-quality storage options, allowing you to save space by compressing images, or full-resolution storage if you prefer.

○ **Access Across Devices**: You can access your backed-up photos on any device by logging into Google Photos with your account, making it easy to view, share, or download images from anywhere.

- **Device Backup**:
  ○ **Backing Up Settings and Apps**: Android allows you to back up device settings, apps, and data to your Google account. Go to **Settings** > **System** > **Backup** and toggle **Back up to Google Drive**. This will save app data, call history, contacts, and settings to Google's cloud.

○ **Automatic and Manual Backups**:
Backups are usually created
automatically, but you can manually
initiate one by tapping "Back up
now." In the event of a device reset
or switch, you can restore data
during setup, reducing the need to
reconfigure everything.

Cloud storage and backup ensure that your data
is secure and accessible, providing peace of
mind in case of loss or damage.

Syncing with Wearable Devices

Android devices are compatible with a variety of
wearables, including smartwatches and fitness
trackers. By syncing a wearable, you can receive
notifications, track health metrics, and control
certain functions from your wrist.

- **Using Wear OS by Google**:
  ○ **Wear OS Basics**: Wear OS is
  Google's operating system for

wearables. It syncs seamlessly with Android phones, allowing you to access notifications, control music, respond to messages, and track fitness metrics.

- ○ **Setting Up Wear OS**: To connect, download the **Wear OS** app on your Android device. Turn on Bluetooth and follow the in-app instructions to pair your wearable. Once connected, you'll have access to various functions directly on your watch.

- ○ **Customizing Notifications and Apps**: You can manage which apps send notifications to your wearable, customize watch faces, and install compatible apps from the Play Store. Wear OS also supports Google Assistant, providing voice commands and reminders directly on your wrist.

- • **Fitness Trackers**:

- ○ **Popular Fitness Apps**: Most fitness trackers, such as those from Fitbit or Garmin, have dedicated apps for Android. Download the appropriate app, create an account, and follow the setup instructions to connect your device.
- ○ **Health and Activity Tracking**: Fitness trackers monitor steps, sleep, heart rate, and even specific workouts. They sync with their respective apps to provide detailed insights into your activity and health trends.
- ○ **Google Fit Integration**: Google Fit is a health platform that can sync with various fitness apps and wearables. It provides a centralized location to view your health and activity data, offering insights into your overall wellness.

Syncing with wearables enhances convenience and allows you to monitor important health and activity metrics without reaching for your phone.

Using Android Auto for Car Integration

Android Auto is designed to bring the power of Android to your car, providing safe access to navigation, music, calls, and more while driving.

- **Setting Up Android Auto**:
    - ○ **Connecting to Your Car**: Android Auto requires a compatible car head unit or an aftermarket display. Connect your Android device using a USB cable (or wirelessly if supported). Your phone will prompt you to open Android Auto, launching a driving-optimized interface on your car's screen.
    - ○ **Wireless Android Auto**: Some newer devices and cars support

wireless Android Auto. To use it, both the phone and the car head unit must support wireless connections. Follow the prompts to set up a wireless connection if supported.

- **Navigation and Maps**:
  - ○ **Google Maps**: With Android Auto, Google Maps becomes easily accessible, providing turn-by-turn directions, live traffic updates, and route options. You can also use voice commands to set destinations, ensuring a hands-free experience.
  - ○ **Waze**: Waze is another popular navigation option available on Android Auto, featuring real-time traffic updates from other drivers, including hazards, speed traps, and alternative routes.
- **Music and Entertainment**:
  - ○ **Supported Media Apps**: Android Auto supports popular music and podcast apps like Spotify, YouTube Music, Audible, and more. You can

control playback using touch or voice commands without distractions.

- ○ **Voice Controls**: Use Google Assistant to play specific songs, podcasts, or playlists, allowing you to stay focused on the road. Simply say, "Play my favorite playlist on Spotify," and Android Auto will handle the rest.
- **Hands-Free Communication**:
  - ○ **Voice-Activated Calls and Messages**: With Android Auto, you can make calls and send messages using voice commands. For example, say "Call Mom" or "Send a message to John," and Android Auto will handle the request, reading incoming messages aloud and allowing you to respond without looking away from the road.
  - ○ **Notification Management**: Android Auto minimizes

notifications to avoid distractions,
only showing essential information
and allowing you to dismiss
non-urgent notifications.

Android Auto transforms your Android device
into a helpful driving assistant, providing
navigation, entertainment, and communication
tools for a safer, more connected experience on
the road.

Staying Safe and Secure

Security is one of the most important aspects of using any mobile device, and Android offers several tools and settings to keep your data and privacy protected. By enabling security features and practicing safe habits, you can significantly reduce the risk of malware, phishing, and other security threats. This section will cover key tools like Google Play Protect, password and biometric security, app permissions, privacy settings, and tips for avoiding online threats.

Google Play Protect and Safe Browsing

Android's Google Play Protect and Safe Browsing features provide a foundational level of security against malicious apps and websites. These tools are integrated directly into the operating system, ensuring they function in the background with minimal user intervention.

- **Google Play Protect**:
  - **What is Google Play Protect?** Google Play Protect is Android's built-in malware protection, designed to scan apps on your device and detect any suspicious or harmful behavior. It checks apps from the Play Store and even scans apps installed from other sources.
  - **How it Works**: Play Protect scans each app on your device periodically, looking for unusual behavior or security risks. If it identifies a potentially harmful app,

it will notify you with the option to uninstall it.

- ○ **Checking Play Protect Settings**: To view Play Protect's status and scan history, go to **Settings > Security > Google Play Protect**. Here, you can enable or disable automatic scanning and review recently scanned apps. It's recommended to keep Play Protect enabled for ongoing protection.

- **Safe Browsing**:
  - ○ **What is Safe Browsing?** Safe Browsing is a feature in Google Chrome that helps protect against malicious websites by warning you when you attempt to visit a potentially dangerous site. It protects against phishing sites, malware downloads, and other online threats.
  - ○ **Activating Safe Browsing**: Safe Browsing is typically enabled by default in the Chrome browser. You

can check or adjust the setting by
opening **Chrome > Settings >
Privacy and security > Safe
Browsing**. You can choose from
different protection levels,
including Enhanced Protection for
increased security.

- **What to Do if You See a Warning**:
If Chrome alerts you about a
potentially harmful website, it's
best to avoid visiting the site. If
you're prompted to download
something, avoid clicking on the
link, as it could contain malware.

Google Play Protect and Safe Browsing offer a
strong foundation for device security by
minimizing exposure to potentially harmful apps
and websites.

Setting Up Passwords and Biometric Security

Setting up strong passwords and enabling biometric security are vital steps to protect your Android device from unauthorized access. Android provides various security options to lock your device and secure sensitive data.

- **Passwords, PINs, and Patterns**:
    - **Choosing a Secure Lock Screen**: Under **Settings** > **Security** > **Screen lock**, you can select from options like Pattern, PIN, or Password. For the highest level of security, a strong alphanumeric password is recommended, as it's more difficult to guess.
    - **Setting a Lock Timeout**: To ensure your device locks automatically, configure the screen timeout under **Settings** > **Display** > **Screen timeout**. A short timeout, such as 30 seconds or one minute,

minimizes the chance of unauthorized access if your device is unattended.

- ○ **Using a PIN or Pattern for App Lock**: Some Android devices offer a built-in option to set additional security for specific apps. Alternatively, you can download third-party apps like AppLock, which enable password protection for individual apps.
- **Biometric Security**:
  - ○ **Fingerprint Unlock**: Most modern Android devices have a fingerprint scanner, allowing you to unlock your phone quickly and securely. To set it up, go to **Settings** > **Security** > **Fingerprint** and follow the instructions to register your fingerprint.
  - ○ **Facial Recognition**: Facial recognition provides a hands-free unlocking option, although it may not be as secure as fingerprint

scanning. To set it up, go to
Settings > **Security** > **Face unlock**
and follow the steps. For best
results, ensure your face is in good
lighting and avoid sunglasses or
hats during setup.

- ○ **Using Biometrics with Apps**:
  Many apps, including banking and
  password manager apps, allow you
  to enable biometric authentication
  for added security. This option is
  usually available within the app's
  security settings, enhancing
  protection for sensitive accounts.

- **Password Manager Integration**:
  - ○ **Using Google Password Manager**:
    Android offers a built-in password
    manager linked to your Google
    account. It saves and autofills
    passwords for supported apps and
    websites. You can access it under
    Settings > **Google** > **Passwords**.
  - ○ **Using Third-Party Password
    Managers**: For added security,

consider a third-party password
manager like LastPass, Dashlane, or
1Password. These apps encrypt
passwords and provide an
additional layer of security for
managing multiple passwords.

By combining a strong screen lock, biometric
security, and a password manager, you can
protect your Android device and accounts from
unauthorized access.

App Permissions and Privacy Settings

App permissions control what information and
features each app can access on your device.
Adjusting these settings is crucial to protect your
privacy and ensure apps only access the
information they need.

- **Reviewing App Permissions**:

○ **Where to Find Permissions**: To view or adjust permissions for individual apps, go to **Settings** > **Privacy** > **Permission manager**. Here, you can see which apps have access to sensitive features, such as the camera, microphone, contacts, and location.

○ **Types of Permissions**: Permissions include access to features like your location, contacts, SMS, microphone, and camera. Only grant necessary permissions to trusted apps and consider whether each permission is essential for the app's functionality.

○ **Managing Special Permissions**: Some apps may request additional permissions, such as the ability to draw over other apps, access usage data, or modify system settings. These can be found under **Settings** > **Apps & notifications** > **Special app access**. Review these carefully

and disable any unnecessary
permissions.

- **Using Privacy Settings**:
  - ○ **Android's Privacy Dashboard**:
    Android's Privacy Dashboard
    provides an overview of which apps
    have recently accessed sensitive
    data, such as location, microphone,
    and camera. To access it, go to
    Settings > **Privacy** > **Privacy
    Dashboard**. This helps you monitor
    and control app activity.
  - ○ **Limiting Location Access**: For
    apps that don't need precise
    location, you can grant approximate
    location instead. Go to the app's
    permissions settings, select
    Location, and choose **Allow only
    while using the app** or **Deny** if
    location access isn't necessary.
  - ○ **Turning Off Personalized Ads**:
    Google uses data to personalize ads
    on Android devices, but you can opt
    out of this tracking. Go to **Settings**

> **Privacy** > **Ads** and enable **Opt out of Ads Personalization**.

By managing app permissions and privacy settings, you can control what data apps can access and reduce potential privacy risks.

Tips for Avoiding Malware and Phishing

Malware and phishing are common security threats that can compromise your device, data, and personal information. By following a few best practices, you can avoid falling victim to these attacks.

- **Avoiding Suspicious Apps and Links**:
  - **Download Apps from Trusted Sources**: Always download apps from reputable sources like the Google Play Store. Avoid installing apps from unknown websites, as they may contain malware. Review

app ratings and read user reviews
for feedback on the app's reliability
and safety.

- **Be Cautious with Email Links**:
  Phishing emails often contain
  malicious links. Avoid clicking on
  any links or downloading
  attachments from unknown senders.
  Instead, verify the sender's email
  address and visit the official
  website directly.
- **Watch for Warning Signs**:
  Phishing messages may contain
  spelling errors, urgent language, or
  unfamiliar URLs. If a message
  seems suspicious, contact the
  organization directly to verify its
  authenticity.

- **Keeping Software Updated**:
  - **Update Android Regularly**:
    System updates often include
    security patches that fix
    vulnerabilities. Go to **Settings** >
    System > **Software update** to

check for updates and keep your
device secure.

- ○ **Enable App Auto-Updates**:
  Updating apps regularly is
  important, as developers often
  release updates to patch security
  flaws. You can enable auto-updates
  in the Google Play Store under
  Settings > **Network preferences** >
  Auto-update apps.
- **Installing Security Apps**:
  - ○ **Consider an Antivirus App**:
    Although Google Play Protect is
    generally sufficient, you may wish
    to add an antivirus app for extra
    protection. Popular options include
    Avast, McAfee, and Norton, which
    provide malware scans and web
    protection.
  - ○ **Using a VPN for Public Wi-Fi**: If
    you frequently use public Wi-Fi,
    consider a VPN (Virtual Private
    Network) for an added layer of
    security. A VPN encrypts your

internet connection, protecting your data from potential hackers on unsecured networks.

- **Avoiding Scams and Phishing Attacks**:
  - **Watch for Fake Websites and Apps**: Fake websites often mimic official ones to trick you into providing personal information. Always check the URL to ensure you're on a legitimate site.
  - **Don't Share Sensitive Information**: Avoid entering sensitive information like passwords, credit card details, or Social Security numbers on suspicious sites or in response to unsolicited emails or messages.
  - **Enable Two-Factor Authentication (2FA)**: Many apps and services offer 2FA as an extra layer of protection. It requires a second form of verification, like a code sent to your phone, ensuring that even if someone knows your

password, they cannot access your account without the second factor.

Getting the Most Out of Google Assistant

Google Assistant is a powerful voice-activated AI tool that can help you manage your tasks, control smart devices, search the web, and more, all from the convenience of your Android device. Whether you're a beginner or an experienced user, this guide will help you maximize the utility of Google Assistant, making your daily life easier and more efficient.

Setting Up and Customizing Google Assistant

Before you can start using Google Assistant to its full potential, it needs to be set up and customized according to your needs and preferences.

- **Activating Google Assistant**:
  - **Voice Activation**: The first step is enabling the voice feature so you can interact with Google Assistant hands-free. Open the **Google Assistant** app, then tap on your profile picture in the upper-right corner. Select **Assistant settings** > **Voice Match** and toggle on the "Hey Google" option to allow voice activation. Once set up, you can simply say "Hey Google" or "OK Google" to start a conversation.
  - **Button Activation**: You can also activate Google Assistant by pressing and holding the home

button (if you use gesture navigation, this will be the middle of the bottom edge) or swipe up from the bottom corner on newer devices.

- **Customizing Google Assistant's Voice and Language**:
  - ○ **Changing the Voice**: In the **Assistant settings**, you can choose between different voices for Google Assistant. You can change the voice's gender, language, and accent. To do this, open **Settings** > **Assistant** > **Voice** and select your preferred voice.
  - ○ **Setting the Language**: You can choose multiple languages to speak with Google Assistant. Go to **Settings** > **Assistant** > **Languages**, where you can add or change your default language(s). This is particularly helpful for bilingual users or those who prefer to use

Google Assistant in a different
language.

- **Customizing Assistant Settings**:
  - ○ **Personalization**: Google Assistant
    can be personalized to offer tailored
    responses based on your
    preferences. For example, you can
    provide your home address, work
    address, and family details to get
    location-based reminders or
    recommendations. To update
    personal info, go to **Assistant
    settings** > **Personal info**.
  - ○ **Notifications**: You can also
    customize which notifications you
    receive from Google Assistant. Go
    to **Settings** > **Notifications** and
    choose from different types of alerts
    such as daily briefings, reminders,
    or sports scores.

Voice Commands and Smart Home Integration

Google Assistant's most powerful feature is its voice commands. Once set up, it can help you control your Android device, perform searches, play media, and even integrate with your smart home devices.

- **Voice Commands for Everyday Tasks**:
  - **Making Calls and Sending Texts**: Use commands like, "Call [contact name]" or "Send a message to [contact name]," followed by the message you want to send. You can also ask it to read your messages aloud.
  - **Setting Alarms and Timers**: Google Assistant can set alarms, timers, or reminders with just a voice command. Try saying, "Set an alarm for 7 AM" or "Set a timer for 10 minutes."

- ○ **Getting Weather Updates**: For quick weather updates, ask, "What's the weather like today?" or "Do I need an umbrella?"
- ○ **Navigation and Traffic**: Ask Google Assistant for directions or traffic conditions, such as "Navigate to [destination]" or "How long will it take to get to work?"
- ○ **Controlling Music and Media**: Control your music, podcasts, or video streaming apps with commands like "Play some jazz music" or "Play the latest episode of my podcast on Spotify."
- ○ **Setting Reminders**: Set time-based or location-based reminders with commands like "Remind me to call Mom at 3 PM" or "Remind me to buy milk when I leave work."
- **Smart Home Integration**:
  - ○ **Setting Up Smart Devices**: If you have smart home devices (e.g., lights, thermostats, speakers), you

can control them with your voice. To integrate a smart device with Google Assistant, go to **Settings** > **Google Assistant** > **Home control**. Follow the prompts to link supported smart devices from brands like Nest, Philips Hue, or Sonos.

- **Controlling Smart Lights**: After setup, you can say, "Turn on the living room lights," "Dim the bedroom lights to 50%," or "Set the lights to blue."
- **Adjusting Smart Thermostats**: Use Google Assistant to change your thermostat settings: "Set the temperature to 72 degrees" or "Increase the temperature by 5 degrees."
- **Voice-Controlled Speakers and TVs**: If you have a smart speaker or smart TV (like Chromecast), you can control media playback or volume by saying, "Pause the TV,"

"Turn the volume up," or "Play Netflix on the living room TV."

Integrating Google Assistant with your smart home devices helps automate and streamline your daily tasks, making your environment more responsive and efficient.

Using Routines and Reminders

Google Assistant can automate your daily activities through **routines** and **reminders**, which help keep you on track and save time.

- **Creating and Using Routines**:
    - ○ **What Are Routines?**: Routines are preset groups of actions that Google Assistant performs with a single command. For example, you could set a "Good morning" routine that tells you the weather, your calendar events, and turns on your smart lights.

○ **Setting Up a Routine**: To create a custom routine, go to **Settings** > **Assistant** > **Routines**. From there, tap the + button to create a new routine, and select the actions you want Google Assistant to perform. You can set specific triggers, such as "Good morning" or "I'm home," and link it to a series of tasks like adjusting the thermostat, playing news updates, or reading the day's schedule.

○ **Example Routines**:

■ *"Good morning"*: Google can tell you the weather, read your calendar, and play your favorite playlist.

■ *"Bedtime"*: Turn off smart lights, set an alarm, and play soothing sounds.

■ *"Leaving home"*: Adjust the thermostat, lock the doors, and play a podcast or music while you drive.

- **Setting Reminders**:
  - **Location-Based Reminders**:
    Google Assistant can remind you to
    do things when you reach specific
    locations. For example, you can say,
    "Remind me to pick up groceries
    when I leave work." You'll get the
    reminder once you are close to your
    designated location.
  - **Time-Based Reminders**: Use
    commands like, "Remind me to call
    the dentist at 2 PM" or "Remind me
    to take my medication every day at
    9 AM."
  - **Recurring Reminders**: You can
    also set recurring reminders like,
    "Remind me to check emails every
    morning at 8 AM."

Routines and reminders can help organize your
day, automate common tasks, and ensure you
never forget important activities.

Fun and Lesser-Known Features of Google Assistant

Google Assistant offers much more than basic tasks and smart home control. Here are some fun and lesser-known features to explore:

- **Entertainment and Fun Commands**:
    - **Jokes and Trivia**: Ask Google Assistant to tell you a joke, "Tell me a joke," or play trivia games, "Let's play trivia."
    - **Games and Activities**: Google Assistant can also play interactive games. Try saying, "Let's play 20 questions," "Play a trivia game," or "Play a game of Jeopardy!"
    - **Easter Eggs**: Google Assistant is packed with hidden Easter eggs. Ask, "What is the meaning of life?" or "Do you like Star Wars?" for some fun, quirky responses.
- **Language Skills**:

- ○ **Learn New Languages**: Google Assistant can teach you phrases in different languages. Ask, "How do you say 'hello' in French?" or "Teach me Spanish."
- ○ **Translate in Real-Time**: You can use Google Assistant for live translation of conversations. Ask, "Translate 'How are you?' into Spanish," or simply say, "Help me speak Spanish."
- **Tracking and Personalized Services**:
  - ○ **Personalized News Briefing**: Google Assistant can give you a custom news briefing based on your interests. Ask, "What's my daily briefing?" and Google will read you personalized news, weather, and traffic updates.
  - ○ **Track Packages**: If you've made an online purchase, Google Assistant can track your orders. Just ask, "Where's my package from Amazon?"

- ○ **Flight Information**: Google Assistant can also give you flight updates. Ask, "What's the status of my flight to New York?" and it will provide real-time information.
- **Sending Money and Making Payments**:
  - ○ **Google Pay Integration**: If you have Google Pay set up, you can send money via Google Assistant by saying, "Send $20 to [contact name] on Google Pay." You can also check your payment history and account balance with commands like, "Check my bank balance."
- **Google Lens Integration**:
  - ○ **Using Google Lens with Assistant**: You can use Google Lens to identify objects, text, and even translate signs or menus in real-time. Ask Google Assistant, "What's this?" while pointing your camera at something, and it will use Google Lens to identify the object.

These fun features and hidden gems make Google Assistant not just a tool for productivity, but a source of entertainment and interaction.

Managing Apps and Storage

Effective management of apps and storage is crucial for keeping your Android device running smoothly and ensuring you have enough space for all your files, photos, and important apps. In this section, you will learn how to install and update apps, manage your storage to avoid running out of space, and use external storage options to expand your device's capacity.

Installing, Updating, and Deleting Apps

Managing apps involves installing new ones, keeping them updated, and removing those that are no longer needed.

- **Installing Apps**:
  - **From Google Play Store**: The easiest and safest way to install apps is through the **Google Play Store**. Open the Play Store app, use the search bar to find the app you want, and tap **Install**. Once installed, you can open the app directly from the Play Store or find it in your home screen or app drawer.
  - **From Third-Party Sources**: You can install apps from sources other than the Play Store, but this comes with risks. To install from third-party sources, go to **Settings** > **Security** > **Install unknown apps**,

and allow your browser or file manager to install apps. Always be cautious when downloading from unofficial sources to avoid malware.

○ **App Suggestions**: The Play Store also provides personalized app recommendations based on your usage patterns and preferences. You can explore these under the **For You** or **Categories** section.

- **Updating Apps**:
  ○ **Automatic Updates**: By default, Android is set to update apps automatically from the Google Play Store. To check or adjust this setting, go to **Google Play Store** > **Settings** > **Auto-update apps**, and choose from options like "Over any network" or "Over Wi-Fi only" to save mobile data.
  ○ **Manual Updates**: You can manually update apps by opening the Play Store, tapping on your

profile picture, selecting **Manage apps & device**, and choosing **Updates available**. You can then tap **Update all** or update specific apps.

- ○ **Checking for App Updates**: Regular updates ensure that apps run smoothly and securely. Developers release updates to fix bugs, introduce new features, and enhance security. It's a good idea to periodically check for app updates, especially if you encounter issues with an app.

- **Deleting Apps**:
  - ○ **From the Home Screen or App Drawer**: To uninstall an app, tap and hold the app icon on your home screen or app drawer, and select **Uninstall** from the pop-up menu. You can also go to **Settings** > **Apps & notifications** > **See all apps**, choose the app you want to uninstall, and select **Uninstall**.

o **Freeing Up Storage**: If your device is running low on space, uninstalling apps you no longer need is one of the fastest ways to free up room. Apps with large data caches, such as games or media apps, often take up significant storage. Removing these can help reclaim space.

o **Removing Bloatware**: Some Android phones come with pre-installed apps (bloatware) that you can't always remove, but you can **disable** them. Go to **Settings > Apps & notifications > See all apps,** select the app, and tap **Disable**. Disabling apps prevents them from running and consuming system resources without fully uninstalling them.

Organizing and Freeing Up Space

Over time, your device may accumulate files, apps, and data that take up valuable storage. This section discusses strategies to help you organize and optimize storage space.

- **Managing App Storage**:
  - **Viewing App Storage Usage**: To check how much space apps are using, go to **Settings** > **Storage** > **Apps**. This shows the storage used by each app, including its data and cache. Some apps, particularly media-heavy ones like social media or messaging apps, can take up significant storage.
  - **Clearing Cache and Data**: Apps store temporary data in caches to speed up loading times. Over time, these caches can grow large and take up unnecessary space. To clear cache or data, go to **Settings** > **Apps & notifications** > **See all apps** > select the app > **Storage & cache**, and then tap **Clear Cache** or

Clear Storage. Note that clearing **Storage** will reset the app, erasing all saved data, settings, and login information.

- **Freeing Up Storage**:
    - **Deleting Unused Files**: Go through your files and delete any that you no longer need. Photos, videos, documents, and downloads can accumulate over time. Open the **Files** app or a file manager app to review and delete unnecessary files.
    - **Using Google Photos for Backups**: Google Photos is a great way to back up photos and videos without taking up local storage. By enabling **Backup & Sync**, you can store an unlimited number of photos and videos (in compressed form) on Google's cloud. After backing them up, you can delete them from your device to free up space.
    - **Managing Downloads**: Files in your **Downloads** folder often pile

up without you realizing. Regularly clean out the folder by opening **Files** > **Downloads**, and delete any files you no longer need.

- **Using Google's "Free Up Space" Tool**:
  - ○ **Optimizing Storage**: Google offers a storage management tool that helps you quickly identify files you can delete. To access this tool, go to **Settings** > **Storage** > **Free up space**. Google will suggest files to delete, such as cached data, old photos, videos, and unused apps.

Introduction to Device Maintenance Tools

Android provides several built-in tools to help optimize and maintain your device's performance, especially when it comes to storage management and overall system health.

- **Device Care and Performance**:

- ○ **Battery and Performance
  Optimization**: Android devices
  come with a built-in **Battery**
  section in settings, where you can
  monitor battery health and
  performance. Go to **Settings** >
  Battery to check battery usage by
  apps and turn on **Battery saver** to
  extend battery life.
- ○ **Device Performance**: Some
  Android devices, particularly
  Samsung phones, include a **Device
  care** feature that helps optimize
  storage, memory, battery, and
  security. Access it by going to
  Settings > **Device care** and tap
  Optimize Now to free up memory
  and improve overall device
  performance.
- **Storage Management and
  Optimization**:
  - ○ **Memory Management**: Under
    Settings > **Storage**, you can find
    tools to optimize storage and

memory. Android will often recommend actions like removing junk files, uninstalling unused apps, or clearing up unnecessary data to improve device performance.

- **Smart Storage**: Some Android versions come with a feature called **Smart Storage**, which automatically frees up space by removing old photos and videos that have been backed up to the cloud. This is particularly useful for users who take a lot of pictures but don't want to manually manage their storage.

- **Security and System Updates**:
  - **System Updates**: Keeping your device updated is important for both security and performance. Go to **Settings** > **System** > **Software update** to check for and install updates. These updates can improve system performance, fix bugs, and patch security vulnerabilities.

○ **Security Updates**: Regular security patches ensure your device is protected against the latest threats. To check for updates, go to **Settings > Security > Security updates**.

Using External Storage (SD Cards, USB Drives)

To expand the storage capacity of your Android device, you can use external storage devices like SD cards or USB drives. This can help you store more photos, videos, music, and documents without taking up internal space.

- **Using SD Cards**:
    - ○ **Inserting and Configuring an SD Card**: Most Android devices come with an SD card slot. To insert the SD card, locate the card slot (usually on the side or under the back cover), insert the card, and restart your device. Once the SD

card is inserted, go to **Settings** > **Storage** to manage it. You can choose to **Format as internal storage** (which encrypts and uses it for apps and data) or **Format as portable storage** (which is used solely for media like photos and music).

○ **Moving Apps to SD Card**: If you have an SD card formatted as **internal storage**, you can move apps and their data to the card. Go to **Settings** > **Apps & notifications** > **See all apps** > select the app > **Storage** > **Change** (if available). You'll be given the option to move the app to the SD card, freeing up internal storage.

- **Using USB Drives**:
  ○ **USB OTG (On-the-Go)**: Android devices with USB-C or micro-USB ports can connect to USB flash drives or external hard drives using a USB OTG adapter. Once plugged

in, you can access the drive through the **Files** app. Simply tap the USB drive option to view and transfer files between your device and the drive.

○ **Copying Files to and from USB**: Use your USB drive to copy large files such as videos, documents, or music from your Android device to free up internal storage, or vice versa to move data onto your device. You can also use file manager apps to facilitate file transfers.

Introduction to Media and Entertainment on Android

Android devices are equipped with powerful tools and features that allow you to manage and enjoy a wide range of media and entertainment content. Whether you're capturing memories with your phone's camera, enjoying music and videos, sharing content on social media, or playing mobile games, Android provides a rich ecosystem for media consumption and creation. In this section, we'll explore the essential features for using media and entertainment apps on Android devices.

Using the Camera and Photo Editing Basics

The camera on Android smartphones has evolved to offer high-quality photos and videos, with many devices featuring multiple lenses and advanced features like night mode, portrait mode, and AI-enhanced photography. Additionally, Android provides a variety of photo-editing apps that let you enhance, adjust, and share your media.

- **Using the Camera**:
  - **Basic Features**: Open your camera app (usually accessed by tapping the camera icon on your home screen or lock screen). Most cameras come with several modes, including **Photo**, **Video**, **Portrait**, **Night Mode**, and sometimes **Pro**

Mode. Use the on-screen buttons to adjust settings like flash, focus, and timer.

- ○ **Zooming**: Most Android cameras allow zooming using pinch gestures. Some high-end models offer optical zoom or hybrid zoom, which allows for better-quality zooming without pixelation.

- ○ **Portrait Mode**: This feature blurs the background to focus on the subject, creating a "bokeh" effect. It's ideal for taking professional-looking photos of people and objects.

- ○ **Night Mode**: When lighting conditions are low, night mode automatically enhances the brightness and detail of your photos without increasing noise, giving you clearer and more vibrant photos at night or in dim environments.

- ● **Photo Editing Basics**:

○ **Editing Photos**: After taking a photo, you can edit it within the camera app or use a third-party photo-editing app like **Snapseed**, **Adobe Lightroom**, or **VSCO**. Basic editing tools include:

- **Crop**: Trim or change the aspect ratio of your photo to focus on the subject or create a better composition.

- **Adjust Brightness and Contrast**: Modify the exposure, shadows, highlights, and contrast to make your photos more visually appealing.

- **Filters and Effects**: Add filters to enhance colors or give your photos a particular style. You can experiment with vibrant, black-and-white, or vintage filters.

- **Retouching**: Some apps provide retouching tools to remove blemishes, adjust skin tones, and even blur or sharpen parts of the image.
- **Text and Stickers**: Add captions, emojis, and stickers to personalize your photos before sharing them.

- **Creating Galleries and Albums**:
  - Many Android devices automatically organize your photos by date and location using **Google Photos**. You can also create custom albums to organize images by events, themes, or people. This feature makes it easy to find and share specific photos.

Managing Music, Videos, and Streaming Apps

Android provides a comprehensive media experience, allowing you to manage and enjoy your music, videos, and streaming content. With support for a wide variety of apps, you can listen to music offline, stream videos, and watch your favorite shows and movies wherever you go.

- **Managing Music**:
  - ○ **Music Apps**: There are several music apps available on Android that let you manage your music library and stream your favorite songs. Popular apps include:
    - ■ **Google Play Music** (now merged with YouTube Music): Play your own music collection, create playlists, and stream millions of tracks.
    - ■ **Spotify**: One of the most popular music streaming platforms, offering a large

catalog of music, podcasts, and playlists.

- **Apple Music**: Apple's music service is available on Android, letting you stream music, discover new releases, and share playlists.

- **SoundCloud**: Stream independent artists' tracks or upload your own music to share.

○ **Downloading Music for Offline Listening**: Many music streaming services allow you to download songs or playlists to listen to offline. In Spotify, for example, you can download your favorite albums or playlists and enjoy them without using data.

○ **Creating Playlists**: Organize your music into playlists. Whether you're creating a workout playlist, road trip playlist, or personal favorites,

you can easily create and share
playlists across different apps.

- **Managing Videos**:
  - ○ **Video Playback**: Android devices
    come with a built-in **Video Player**
    that supports various video formats,
    including MP4, AVI, MKV, and
    more. You can watch videos
    directly from the device's storage or
    stream from apps.
  - ○ **YouTube**: As the most popular
    video platform, YouTube provides
    an endless supply of content. The
    YouTube app allows you to watch,
    like, and share videos, as well as
    subscribe to your favorite channels.
    Premium users can download
    videos and enjoy an ad-free
    experience.
  - ○ **Other Streaming Platforms**: Other
    popular video streaming services
    include:

- **Netflix**: Watch movies and TV shows, including exclusive originals.
- **Disney+**: Stream Disney content, including Pixar, Marvel, Star Wars, and National Geographic.
- **Amazon Prime Video**: Stream a wide variety of movies and shows, including Prime-exclusive content.

- **Streaming Music and Video**:
  - **Cast to Your TV**: Android devices can connect to smart TVs or streaming devices like **Chromecast**, allowing you to cast content directly from your device to the big screen.
  - **Live Streaming**: Apps like **Twitch**, **YouTube Live**, and **Facebook Live** let you stream live content to an audience. Whether you're broadcasting yourself or watching others, live streaming has become a

major part of social media and
entertainment.

Creating and Sharing Content on Social Media

Android devices are designed to help you create,
share, and consume content across various social
media platforms. The ability to easily capture
photos and videos, edit them on the go, and
share them instantly with friends and followers
has revolutionized how we interact online.

- **Taking Photos and Videos for Social Media**:
  - Most social media platforms like **Instagram, Facebook, Twitter,** and **TikTok** allow users to upload content directly from the camera app or photo gallery. Use filters and effects to enhance your content and make it more engaging.

- ○ **Instagram Stories and Reels**:
  Create short video clips or images
  that disappear after 24 hours
  (Stories), or post short, engaging
  videos (Reels) to share with your
  followers. These features encourage
  frequent content creation and allow
  you to share in real-time.
- ○ **TikTok**: TikTok is a unique
  platform for creating and sharing
  short-form video content. The
  in-app video editor allows you to
  add effects, music, and text to your
  videos, making it one of the most
  creative social apps.
- **Sharing on Social Media**:
  - ○ **Sharing from Apps**: Android has
    built-in sharing features that let you
    send content directly to social
    media apps. From the **Gallery**,
    Photos, or **Camera** app, you can
    select the media you want to share
    and choose the platform you want
    to post it on.

- o **Hashtags and Tagging**: Use hashtags (#) to make your content discoverable by a wider audience, and tag people or brands to engage with others. Hashtags help increase the visibility of your posts on platforms like Twitter and Instagram.
  - o **Story Highlights**: On Instagram, you can save your Stories to a permanent section called "Highlights" on your profile, so your best content remains visible long after the 24-hour expiration.
- **Engaging with Followers**:
  - o **Comments and Direct Messages**: Respond to comments on your posts to engage with your followers. Most platforms also allow private messaging, where you can chat one-on-one with friends or followers.
  - o **Live Streaming**: Social media platforms like Instagram, Facebook,

and YouTube allow you to go live, enabling followers to interact with you in real-time.

Tips for Enjoying Mobile Games on Android

Mobile gaming on Android has evolved to offer rich, immersive experiences that rival console and PC games. Whether you're into casual games or complex strategy games, Android offers something for everyone.

- **Finding and Installing Games**:
    - **Google Play Store**: The Play Store is home to a vast library of games across all genres, from puzzle games to action-packed shooters. Popular game categories include **Casual**, **Racing**, **Adventure**, **Sports**, and **Role-playing (RPG)**.
    - **Game Recommendations**: The Play Store also provides

personalized game recommendations based on your play history and interests. You can browse the **Top Charts** or explore **Editor's Choice** games for the best-rated games.

- **Enhancing Your Gaming Experience**:
  - **Graphics and Settings**: Many Android games allow you to adjust graphics settings for better performance or visual quality. Lowering the resolution can improve performance on lower-end devices, while high-end devices can offer smooth, high-definition graphics.
  - **Game Controllers**: If you prefer using a physical controller, Android supports Bluetooth game controllers. Pairing a controller can provide a more traditional gaming experience, especially for console-style games.
- **Multiplayer and Online Gaming**:

○ **Online Games**: Android is home to a variety of multiplayer games like **PUBG Mobile**, **Fortnite**, and **Call of Duty Mobile**, where you can team up with or compete against players worldwide.

○ **In-app Purchases**: Many games offer in-app purchases for extra lives, characters, or power-ups. Be cautious when making purchases and ensure that parental controls are in place if children are using your device.

Productivity Tools and Tips on Android

Android devices are powerful tools for productivity, enabling you to manage tasks, communicate effectively, and streamline your work processes on the go. Whether you're handling emails, managing documents, or multitasking between apps, Android offers a variety of features and apps to boost your efficiency. In this section, we will explore essential productivity tools and tips to help you maximize your Android device for work and everyday tasks.

Setting Up Email and Productivity Apps

Email is an essential tool for communication, and Android provides several options for managing your emails efficiently. Productivity apps, such as task managers, note-taking tools, and calendar apps, help you stay organized and on track throughout the day. Let's explore how to set up and optimize these tools.

- **Setting Up Email**:
  - **Gmail**: As the default email service on Android, Gmail is a robust tool for managing both personal and professional email accounts. Setting up Gmail is simple:
    1. Open the **Gmail** app.
    2. If it's your first time, tap **Add an email address**, and choose the type of account (Google, Outlook, Yahoo, etc.).

3. Enter your login credentials for the chosen service and follow the prompts.

4. After setup, you can access your inbox, compose emails, and organize your messages into folders.

○ **Managing Multiple Accounts**: Gmail allows you to link multiple email accounts to the app, so you can switch between work, personal, and other email addresses seamlessly. To manage accounts:

1. Open Gmail.

2. Tap your profile picture in the top right corner and choose **Add another account**.

3. Log in to the new account, and you can toggle between accounts from the same interface.

○ **Email Management**: Use labels, folders, and filters to categorize incoming emails. Mark important messages with stars or flags to keep track of tasks and priorities. Set up automatic responses for vacation or out-of-office replies.

- **Productivity Apps**: Android offers a range of apps designed to help you stay organized and productive, from managing tasks to taking notes:
  - **Google Keep**: A simple and powerful note-taking app that allows you to create text, voice, and photo notes, set reminders, and organize your ideas. You can even collaborate on notes with others in real-time.
  - **Microsoft Office Suite**: The Microsoft Office apps—**Word, Excel, PowerPoint**—are available on Android, allowing you to create, edit, and collaborate on documents, spreadsheets, and presentations while on the go.

o **Google Drive**: Google Drive allows you to store, share, and collaborate on documents and files in real-time. It integrates seamlessly with other Google services, making it easy to access files from any device.

o **Trello or Asana**: For team project management and personal task tracking, tools like **Trello** and **Asana** provide visual boards and task lists. These apps help you organize work, set deadlines, assign tasks, and monitor progress in both personal and collaborative projects.

Managing Documents and Files on Android

Android makes it easy to manage documents, files, and media across your device and in the cloud. Whether you're dealing with PDFs, Word documents, or multimedia content, effective file management can help keep your workflow efficient and organized.

- **Managing Files on Android**:
  - ○ **File Manager**: Android devices come with a built-in file manager (often called **Files** or **My Files**) that lets you browse, organize, and manage files stored on your device. You can move, delete, copy, and share files directly from the file manager.
    - ■ **Creating Folders**: To organize your files, create folders by tapping the three-dot menu in the top corner of the file manager and selecting "New Folder." You can name the folder and move relevant files into it for easier access.
    - ■ **Searching for Files**: The file manager allows you to search for files by name or type.

This is particularly useful when you have a large volume of files and need to locate something quickly.

- ○ **Cloud Storage**:
  - ■ **Google Drive**: Google's cloud storage service gives you 15 GB of free space to store documents, photos, videos, and other files. You can easily upload files from your device and access them across devices using your Google account.
  - ■ **Dropbox or OneDrive**: Other popular cloud storage options, like **Dropbox** and **Microsoft OneDrive**, also offer Android apps for file syncing and sharing.
- ○ **File Sharing**: You can share files directly from the file manager or any other app by selecting the file and tapping the share icon. You can

send files via email, messaging apps, Bluetooth, or cloud services.

- **Document Editing**:
    - ○ **Google Docs**: For word processing, **Google Docs** is a versatile tool. You can create, edit, and collaborate on documents in real-time. Google Docs supports voice typing, so you can dictate your document rather than typing it out.
    - ○ **PDF Management**: If you deal with PDF documents frequently, consider installing an app like **Adobe Acrobat Reader** to view, annotate, and sign PDF files. You can also use it to convert PDFs to other formats like Word or Excel.

Using Split-Screen and Picture-in-Picture Mode

Android offers several multitasking features that allow you to be more productive by using multiple apps simultaneously. These tools let you view or interact with two or more apps at once, making it easier to manage tasks and information.

- **Split-Screen Mode**: Split-Screen Mode allows you to run two apps simultaneously on your screen. This feature is especially useful for tasks like referencing a document while writing an email or browsing the web while taking notes.
  - **Activating Split-Screen**:
    1. Open the first app you want to use.
    2. Tap the **Recent Apps** button (usually the square button in the navigation bar).
    3. Find the app you want to use and tap the app icon at the top of the preview.
    4. Select **Split screen** from the options. Your app will be pinned to the top or left half of the screen.

5. Choose a second app from the Recent Apps list or open it from your home screen.

○ **Adjusting App Sizes**: After the apps are placed in split-screen mode, you can drag the divider between them to adjust their sizes. Some apps, like YouTube, may have limited functionality in split-screen mode, so you might not always get a perfect experience.

● **Picture-in-Picture Mode (PiP)**: PiP mode is a handy feature for watching videos while performing other tasks. You can watch a video in a small floating window while using another app.

○ **Using PiP Mode**:

1. Open a video in an app like **YouTube**, **Google Maps**, or **Netflix**.

2. Tap the home button to minimize the video. The video will shrink into a

floating window that you can move around the screen.

3. Resize the floating window by dragging the edges or use the built-in controls to pause or close the video.

○ **PiP App Support**: Not all apps support PiP, but many popular video and video call apps like **YouTube, Google Duo**, and **Netflix** do. PiP is especially useful for multitasking and handling calls or other tasks while watching videos.

Top Productivity Apps to Enhance Your Workflow

To take your productivity to the next level, Android offers a range of apps designed to help you stay organized, efficient, and focused. These apps can assist with managing tasks, projects, time, and collaboration.

- **Task Management Apps**:
  - ○ **Todoist**: This powerful task management app lets you create to-do lists, set deadlines, prioritize tasks, and organize projects. It offers cross-platform syncing, allowing you to stay on top of your tasks from any device.
  - ○ **Microsoft To Do**: Integrated with Microsoft Office, this app offers seamless task management, allowing you to create, prioritize, and set reminders for tasks. It also integrates with Outlook, so your tasks sync automatically with your calendar.
  - ○ **Google Keep**: Google Keep is a simple, easy-to-use note-taking app that syncs with your Google account. It allows you to capture text, voice notes, and images, and organize them with labels and colors.
- **Time Management Apps**:

- ○ **Toggl**: Track the time you spend on various tasks with **Toggl**. It helps you understand where your time goes, making it easier to adjust and be more productive. It's especially useful for freelancers and teams.
- ○ **Forest**: This unique app helps you stay focused by planting a virtual tree that grows as you work without distractions. If you leave the app, the tree dies, encouraging you to stay on task.
- **Note-Taking Apps**:
  - ○ **Evernote**: Evernote is a feature-rich note-taking app that lets you create notes, organize them into notebooks, and add images, attachments, and web clippings. It syncs across all your devices.
  - ○ **OneNote**: Microsoft's **OneNote** is another excellent note-taking app. It offers robust organizational features, including notebooks,

sections, and tags, and integrates well with Microsoft Office.

- **Collaboration Apps**:
  - ○ **Slack**: A team communication and collaboration tool that lets you chat in real-time, organize conversations by channels, share files, and integrate with a range of productivity tools.
  - ○ **Zoom**: For remote meetings and video conferencing, **Zoom** is a popular choice. It lets you set up video calls, webinars, and screen sharing, helping teams stay connected.

Advanced Settings and Troubleshooting on Android

As you become more familiar with Android, you may want to dive deeper into its advanced settings and troubleshooting tools. These features can help you enhance your device's performance, solve technical problems, and access hidden options that aren't readily available in the standard settings. In this section, we'll cover developer options, system updates, troubleshooting common issues, and performing a factory reset.

Developer Options: When and How to Use Them

Developer Options are hidden settings designed primarily for developers, but they can be incredibly useful for power users who want to take more control over their device's behavior. These options allow you to access a variety of tools for debugging, testing, and optimizing your Android experience.

- **Enabling Developer Options**: Developer options are not enabled by default. To turn them on:
  - Go to **Settings** > **About phone**.
  - Scroll down and tap **Build number** seven times. You might be asked to enter your device's lock screen password.
  - After this, you will see a message saying that Developer options have been unlocked.

- ○ Developer options will now appear in your **Settings** menu under **System > Developer options**.
- **Key Developer Options You Might Find Useful**:
  - ○ **USB Debugging**: This option allows you to connect your Android device to a computer for development purposes. It's often used by developers to interact with the device via the Android Debug Bridge (ADB) tool. It's also necessary if you're trying to root your device or flash a custom ROM.
  - ○ **OEM Unlocking**: If you're planning on unlocking your bootloader for custom ROM installations or rooting your device, this option must be enabled. Be cautious, as unlocking the bootloader can void warranties and may result in data loss.

○ **Stay Awake**: This setting keeps your screen on while the device is charging, which can be useful when testing apps or using the device as a console or dashboard.

○ **Window Transition and Animator Duration Scales**: These settings let you speed up or slow down the animation effects when opening apps or transitioning between screens. Decreasing the values can make your phone feel faster, though it may reduce visual appeal.

○ **Mock Locations**: Developers use this setting to test location-based services by simulating different geographical locations. If you're a developer or just curious, this tool can allow you to mock your GPS position.

○ **Force GPU Rendering**: This option forces your device to use GPU for rendering 2D graphics,

which can make certain apps run
smoother. However, it may also
drain your battery faster.

- **When and How to Use Developer
  Options**:
  - ○ **Use Caution**: Many of these
    options are meant for developers or
    advanced users. Enabling or
    changing settings you don't
    understand could result in system
    instability or performance issues.
  - ○ **Stay in Control**: If you ever need
    to disable Developer Options, you
    can simply toggle the switch at the
    top of the Developer Options menu.

Understanding System Updates and Security Patches

Regular updates are vital for keeping your
Android device running smoothly, improving
security, and adding new features.
Understanding how system updates work and

how to manage them is an essential part of device maintenance.

- **Why Updates Matter**:
  - ○ **Bug Fixes**: Updates can fix bugs and glitches that may have been present in previous versions of Android.
  - ○ **Security Patches**: One of the most important reasons to keep your device updated is for security. Updates often include security patches that address vulnerabilities that could be exploited by malicious apps or websites.
  - ○ **New Features**: Some updates also bring new features or improvements to the Android operating system, allowing your device to benefit from the latest technology.
- **How to Check for System Updates**: To check for system updates:
  - ○ Go to **Settings** > **System** > **Software update**.

- o Your device will automatically check for any available updates.
- o If there's an update available, you'll be prompted to download and install it.
- o Tap **Download** and wait for the update to complete. You may need to restart your device for the changes to take effect.
- **Managing Updates**:
    - o **Update Notifications**: Android devices typically notify you when an update is available. You can schedule the update to install during off-hours if you don't want to be interrupted.
    - o **Automating Updates**: Ensure that **Auto-update** is enabled in your **Google Play Store** to keep apps up to date automatically. For system updates, you can set your phone to install updates overnight, or you can manually install them when convenient.

- **Security Patches**: Security patches are crucial for protecting your personal data and privacy. Android updates often address security holes found by Google and other researchers. You can view your security patch level by going to **Settings > About phone > Android version > Security patch level**.

Basic Troubleshooting Steps for Common Issues

From time to time, Android devices can experience issues such as slow performance, app crashes, or connectivity problems. Fortunately, many common problems have simple solutions. Below are some basic troubleshooting steps that can help resolve common issues.

- **Device is Slow or Unresponsive**:
  - **Restart Your Device**: A simple restart can often resolve performance issues by clearing out

temporary files, freeing up memory, and closing background apps.

- ○ **Clear Cache**: Over time, cached data can accumulate and slow down your device. To clear the cache, go to **Settings** > **Storage** > **Cached data** and tap **Clear cache**.

- ○ **Close Unnecessary Apps**: If you have too many apps running in the background, your device can slow down. Use the **Recent Apps** screen to close apps you're not using.

- ○ **Uninstall Unnecessary Apps**: If storage space is full, your device may slow down. Uninstall apps you don't need or use **Storage settings** to free up space by deleting unnecessary files.

- • **Connectivity Issues**:
  - ○ **Wi-Fi Problems**: If you're having trouble connecting to Wi-Fi, try turning Wi-Fi off and on again. Alternatively, restart your router or

forget and reconnect to the Wi-Fi
network.

○ **Bluetooth Not Working**: If your
Bluetooth connection is acting up,
turn Bluetooth off and on again.
You can also try un-pairing and
re-pairing with your device.

○ **Mobile Data Problems**: If your
mobile data is not working, ensure
that **Mobile data** is enabled in
Settings. You can also toggle
Airplane Mode on and off to reset
connections.

• **App Crashes or Freezes**:

○ **Force Close the App**: If an app is
misbehaving, you can force close it
by going to **Settings** > **Apps** >
select the problematic app > **Force
stop**.

○ **Clear App Cache**: Sometimes, an
app's cached data can cause issues.
Go to **Settings** > **Apps** > select the
app > **Storage** > **Clear cache**.

- o **Reinstall the App**: If clearing the cache doesn't help, try uninstalling and reinstalling the app from the **Google Play Store**.
- **Battery Draining Fast**:
  - o **Check Battery Usage**: Go to **Settings** > **Battery** > **Battery usage** to see which apps are using the most power. You can disable or uninstall high-drain apps.
  - o **Power Saving Mode**: Enable **Battery Saver** in **Settings** to limit background processes and extend battery life.
  - o **Screen Brightness**: Reduce the screen brightness or enable **Adaptive brightness** to let your device adjust brightness based on your environment.

Factory Reset and Data Backup

Sometimes, the best way to resolve deep issues with your device—like software bugs, lagging, or persistent app crashes—is to perform a **Factory Reset**. However, this will erase all the data on your device, so it's critical to back up your data before proceeding.

- **Backing Up Your Data**:
    - **Google Backup**: Android devices allow you to back up your data to Google. To back up your data:
        1. Go to **Settings** > **System** > **Backup**.
        2. Ensure that **Back up to Google Drive** is enabled. Your contacts, calendar events, app data, and photos can be backed up to your Google account.
    - **Photos and Videos**: Use **Google Photos** to back up your photos and videos to the cloud. This will keep them safe even after a factory reset.

- o **Other Backup Solutions**: Consider third-party apps like **Dropbox** or **OneDrive** for cloud-based backups of important files.
- **Factory Reset**: If all troubleshooting steps fail and your device continues to have problems, a factory reset may be your last resort. This will wipe your device clean and restore it to its original factory settings.
  - o Go to **Settings** > **System** > **Reset** > **Factory data reset**.
  - o Read the warnings and tap **Reset phone**.
  - o Confirm by entering your PIN or password, and the reset process will begin.
  - o **Note**: A factory reset erases all data on your device, including apps, settings, photos, and personal files. Ensure that your data is backed up before proceeding.

Android Ecosystem: Tips and Resources

The Android ecosystem is vast, offering a variety of tools, apps, websites, and resources to help users get the most out of their devices. Whether you're a beginner or an experienced Android user, there are countless ways to enhance your experience, stay informed, and find support when needed. In this section, we'll explore recommended apps for new users, the best websites and forums for Android tips, staying updated with the latest features, and where to find help and community resources.

Recommended Apps for New Users

As a new Android user, navigating the app landscape can be overwhelming due to the sheer number of options available. However, there are several essential apps that can significantly improve your experience, ranging from productivity tools to entertainment, social media, and utilities. Here are some must-have apps for new Android users:

- **Google Apps**:
    - **Google Play Store**: The hub for downloading and updating apps. It's where you'll find most of the apps you'll need for your device.
    - **Google Chrome**: The default web browser on Android devices, offering fast browsing, synchronization with your Google account, and robust privacy features.
    - **Google Photos**: This app offers unlimited cloud storage for your photos and videos (if you use

Google's compression options) and easy organization features. It's a great backup option for your media.

- ○ **Gmail**: Google's email app that integrates with your Google account for seamless communication and syncs across devices.
- ○ **Google Maps**: One of the best navigation apps, helping you get around with accurate real-time traffic data, turn-by-turn directions, and recommendations for nearby restaurants, shops, and more.
- **Productivity Apps**:
  - ○ **Microsoft Office**: Word, Excel, PowerPoint, and OneNote allow you to work on documents, spreadsheets, and presentations directly from your Android device.
  - ○ **Google Keep**: A note-taking app that lets you quickly jot down ideas, to-do lists, and reminders, which

sync across devices via your Google account.

- ○ **Trello**: A task management app that's ideal for organizing projects and collaborating with others using boards, lists, and cards.
- ○ **Slack**: For teams that need to stay in constant communication, Slack is a popular app for organizing group chats, file sharing, and team collaboration.

- **Social Media and Communication Apps**:
  - ○ **WhatsApp**: A widely-used messaging app that supports text messaging, voice and video calls, and media sharing. It's ideal for keeping in touch with friends and family.
  - ○ **Telegram**: A privacy-focused messaging app with enhanced security features and group chat capabilities.

- ○ **Instagram**: If you enjoy social media and sharing photos, Instagram is one of the most popular platforms for both casual and professional sharing.
  - ○ **Facebook**: Still one of the most widely used social media platforms, Facebook allows you to connect with friends, join groups, and follow your favorite pages.
- **Entertainment Apps**:
  - ○ **Spotify**: One of the best music streaming apps, offering a wide library of songs, playlists, and podcasts.
  - ○ **Netflix**: A leading video streaming service that lets you watch movies, TV shows, and exclusive content directly on your Android device.
  - ○ **YouTube**: The go-to app for video content, from educational tutorials to entertainment. You can watch, share, and even upload your own videos.

- o **Audible**: An audiobook service where you can listen to a massive library of books across genres, ideal for long commutes or exercising.
- **Utilities and Tools**:
  - o **Tasker**: A powerful automation app that allows you to create custom actions based on triggers like time, location, or events.
  - o **LastPass**: A password manager that stores your passwords securely and auto-fills login details for websites and apps.
  - o **Files by Google**: A file management app that makes it easy to manage your downloads, files, and photos, with features to free up space.
  - o **AirDroid**: An app that lets you control and transfer files between your Android device and a computer or another mobile device wirelessly.

These apps cover a broad range of needs and can help you personalize your device, stay productive, and enjoy entertainment seamlessly.

Best Websites, Forums, and YouTube Channels for Android Tips

If you're looking to learn more about Android, troubleshoot issues, or stay informed about the latest developments, several websites, forums, and YouTube channels can be invaluable resources.

- **Websites**:
    - **Android Central**: One of the most popular websites for Android enthusiasts, offering news, reviews, tutorials, and troubleshooting tips. It's a great place to stay updated on the latest trends in the Android world.
    - **XDA Developers**: A renowned community for Android developers

and power users. XDA offers in-depth articles, custom ROMs, kernel mods, and step-by-step guides for unlocking and customizing your Android device.

○ **Android Police**: A great resource for Android news, updates, app reviews, and troubleshooting advice. It provides the latest information about Android OS releases and features.

○ **9to5Google**: A leading source for Android news, Google-related product announcements, and software updates.

○ **PhoneArena**: This site covers a wide range of Android device reviews, comparisons, and news, helping you stay informed about the latest phones and software.

- **Forums**:
  ○ **Reddit's Android Communities**: There are several subreddits dedicated to Android, such as

r/**Android**, r/**AndroidQuestions**, and r/**AndroidDev**. These forums are filled with users and experts sharing tips, solving problems, and discussing the latest Android trends.

- ○ **Android Stack Exchange**: This is a Q&A site specifically for Android-related questions, where users can ask and answer technical questions about Android devices, apps, and software.
- ○ **XDA Developers Forum**: As mentioned, XDA's forum is a go-to place for Android modding, rooting, custom ROMs, and expert-level discussions about advanced Android topics.
- **YouTube Channels**:
  - ○ **MKBHD (Marques Brownlee)**: Marques is one of the top tech influencers on YouTube, offering high-quality reviews and deep dives into the latest Android devices and tech.

- **Unbox Therapy**: Another top YouTuber in the tech world, Unbox Therapy provides detailed, hands-on reviews of the latest Android devices and gadgets, showcasing the pros and cons of each.
- **Android Authority**: Dedicated to all things Android, this channel offers tutorials, reviews, tips, and tricks for Android users at all experience levels.
- **Dave Lee (Dave2D)**: Known for his insightful and balanced reviews, Dave2D offers great analysis on Android devices, with a focus on performance and design.
- **The Verge**: The Verge's YouTube channel covers a wide array of tech news, and its Android-related videos feature product reviews, news, and expert analysis.

Staying Updated with the Latest Android Features

The Android ecosystem is constantly evolving, with new features, updates, and improvements being released regularly. Here's how you can stay on top of the latest developments:

- **Google's Official Blog**: Google often announces new Android features, OS updates, and tips through their official blog. You can also find detailed blog posts on changes made in the latest Android releases.
- **Android Beta Program**: Google offers a **Beta Program** for Android, where users can enroll to receive early access to upcoming versions of the Android OS. By joining, you can test new features before they are released to the public.
- **Tech News Sites**: Websites like **Android Central**, **9to5Google**, and **TechCrunch** regularly cover Android software updates and feature releases. Subscribing to their

newsletters or following them on social media can keep you updated.

- **Social Media**: Following Android-related Twitter accounts and subreddits like **r/Android** can help you stay informed about new apps, updates, and features as soon as they're announced.

- **Google Play Store**: The Play Store often highlights the latest Android apps and new features for popular apps. Checking out the **What's New** section in the Play Store can give you insight into new developments.

Where to Find Help: Support Options and Community Resources

If you ever need help with your Android device, several support options and community resources can provide assistance.

- **Google Support**: Google's official support site offers troubleshooting guides,

FAQs, and live chat support. You can visit
support.google.com to find answers to
common issues related to Android,
Google services, and apps.

- **Device Manufacturer Support**: If you
  have a device from brands like Samsung,
  OnePlus, or Xiaomi, they often provide
  dedicated support channels, including
  online help, phone support, and in-person
  visits at authorized service centers.

- **Android Help Center**: This built-in app
  on many Android devices provides helpful
  guides, tutorials, and frequently asked
  questions on topics like setting up your
  device, managing apps, and
  troubleshooting.

- **Community Forums**: As mentioned
  earlier, sites like **Reddit**, **XDA
  Developers**, and **Android Stack
  Exchange** are fantastic places to ask
  questions, share experiences, and get help
  from fellow Android users.